HANDLING
ROPES & LINES
AFLOAT

HANDLING ROPES & LINES AFLOAT

PAUL AND ARTHUR SNYDER

Nautical

Nautical Publishing Company Limited

Copyright 1967 © by Paul and Arthur Snyder
Revised and enlarged edition 1970
Reprinted 1976

First published in the United States of America
under the title *"Knots and Lines, illustrated"*
by John de Graff Inc, Tuckahoe, 1970

This edition is published in Great Britain by
NAUTICAL PUBLISHING COMPANY
Lymington, Hampshire, England
In association with
George G Harrap & Co Ltd
London, Toronto, Sydney, Wellington

ISBN 0 245 50615 2

Printed offset in England by
The Camelot Press Ltd, Southampton

CONTENTS

INTRODUCTION

The purpose of this manual is to teach a beginner "how" to tie basic knots on board the cruising and racing sailboat (often called an auxiliary). "How" in this article does not mean primarily when, why, or where to apply a knot, or what the knot looks like. These aspects are included as secondary purposes. The most important thing to know is the specific motions the hands must go through in tying the knot. These motions are hard for the beginner to learn and for the experienced sailor to teach.

Another purpose is to provide a ready reference for those who forget. During the long winter months even an old salt might use this information as a basis for developing his own "different ships = different long splices" way of work.

Unfortunately for those of us who are romantics, "marlinspike seamanship" seems to be a thing of the past. Fancy splicing and cockscombing are time-consuming and remain only for the expert of the boat yard. So we concern ourselves here with what the beginner may be required to do on either the port or starboard watch, when racing, or on a Sunday afternoon.

On board a sailboat, knots much be tied quickly and surely, using as few motions as possible. This demands enough practice to be able to visualize the knot clearly. The beginner needs an easily remembered procedure for tying an unfamiliar knot and then enough practice to know the appearance of the knot and the approach to tying it. Once a knot is learned, a minute's refresher brings back proficiency. One must be able to tie each knot without looking so that, when necessary, it can be tied in the dark.

One of the problems the skipper faces with a green crew member is giving effective line handling orders. He knows what he wants, but the novice does not understand. Even making fast the dinghy painter can then become an awkward maneuver. We will also explain basic line handling techniques.

Today lines are made of synthetic fiber (dacron or nylon) or wire. They are resistant to salt water, sunlight, rot, and mildew—the enemies of manila and hemp and other organic fibers. Nylon rope has great elasticity, making it good for anchor rodes and mooring pendants. Dacron, which does not stretch so much as nylon and returns to its original length much faster, makes better line for sheets and halyards. All synthetic fibers are easy to splice, including braided rope. The latter does kink more than "laid up" stranded rope, so that care must be taken in coiling it, especially when it is wet. Since synthetic fibers are almost three times as strong as new manila, they permit smaller lines which are more flexible, take less space to stow, and are easier to handle.

EXPLANATION OF PROCEDURE AND TERMS USED

Where practical each knot and each line handling operation has:

1. A brief general description.
2. An outline of a typical use with an illustration—not the only use, of course.
3. A specific description, numbered step by step, of how to tie the knot or how to perform the operation, with corresponding numbered illustrations.

The camera has been located as close to where your eye will be as is possible. Therefore, the descriptions are addressed to how the operation will look to you as you tie the knot looking down on the work. "To the rear" means "away from you," but in some pictures "up" might be more appropriate.

Remember, knots should be tied boldly and quickly with the hands—not daintily with the fingers. When you can tie a knot with your eyes closed, teach the knot to another person, then you will know it! Use any piece of rope you have. Clothes line will do quite well. Work through each description step by step. RH and LH denote right and left hand.

We have tried to keep nautical terminology to a minimum, using it without definition in the text only where a lack of complete understanding would not detract from our objective—describing tying knots and handling lines. However, as soon as you go aboard, the language of the sea will be used as it has been for centuries. It is precise and picturesque, and we believe that including some will be more helpful than confusing. The Glossary (page 95) defines terms with special nautical meaning.

To the sailor, almost all ropes are called "lines." The few exceptions,* such as manrope, footrope, are not often used on modern yachts. Many sails have a boltrope along the luff, foot, and sometimes the leech; but since this rope is an integral part of the sail, it is not subject to line handling. Wire rope is usually called "wire rope" or just "wire."

We define the terms we use in describing knots and line handling on the following four pages. A *knot* is formed in the line itself, such as the Figure of Eight. *Bends* join two lines, *Hitches* bend a line to a spar, ring, or other line. There are exceptions and contradictions since the terminology comes from different seagoing services and nationalities.

*Complete list under Rope in Glossary.

BASIC TERMS

As you read, practice with a piece of line so that you will become accustomed to the terminology.

We suggest that the novice begin with the uncomplicated Half Hitch, Figure of Eight, or Reef Knot. Learning to tie knots requires patience and persistence. Proceed one step at a time, making sure to follow the illustrations. A false step can be most frustrating since the knot cannot be tied.

1. *End—The way we will use it—the last foot or two of the line. The Bitter End will be the last six inches of line.*

2. *Standing Part—The part of the line which leads from the knot being tied toward the load.*

3. *Bight—Bend or loop in the line. A Closed Bight will signify that the line crosses itself in forming the Bight. An Open Bight is formed when a loop is made without the line crossing itself.*

4. *Nip—The part or parts of the knot where the line itself or another line brings pressure to provide the friction that makes the knot hold. The better knots do not have a nip which jams. A good knot can be untied as fast as it is tied.*

5. *Fixed Object—For the purpose of this handbook only, it is the ring, spar, cleat, bitt, other line, etc., to which the line is being tied. It is not a nautical term.*

6. *Turn—Single "wrap" of a line around another line or spar, etc., which reverses the direction of haul by 180°.*

7. *Round Turn—A full turn. Actually more than 360° of line may contact the fixed object.*

8. *Slack—Looseness in a line. It may be in the knot itself or anywhere in the line. Also used as a verb.*

FIGURE OF EIGHT

The simplest of stopper knots.

Use To prevent a line from unreeving through a block, fairlead, or cleat eye.

To tie

1. *With 8'' End in RH, cross back over Standing Part to form a Closed Bight.*

2. *Reach under Standing Part with RH and pull End under and around Standing Part. Bring up outside of Bight.*

3. *With RH tuck End back down through Closed Bight.*

4. *Work knot snug, but do not jam.*

5. *To add bulk, several Round Turns may be taken after Step 2. It is then called a Stevedore Knot.*

HALF HITCH

A simple knot being a form of the Overhand Knot.

Use Basis for several other knots. It is not secure by itself and is only used alone for the most temporary hitch.

To tie

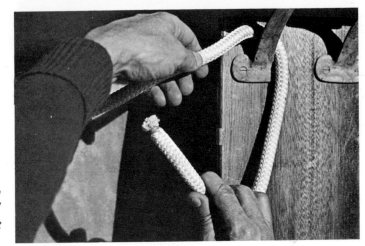

1. *With RH take a Turn around Fixed Object with 1' of End. Hold Standing Part in LH.*

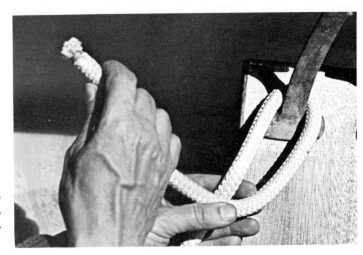

2. *With RH pull End up and over Standing Part to the left. Hold End with left thumb.*

3. *With RH reach through Bight and pull End back through.*

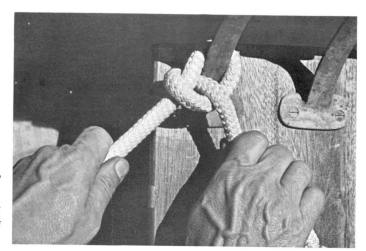

4. *Pull up snug. Where quick untying is more important than security, a knot may be slipped. The Half Hitch is often slipped.*

To slip

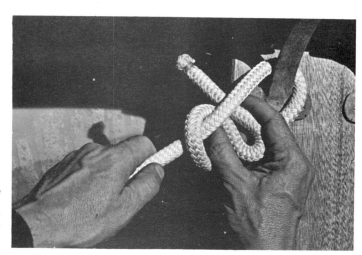

5. *Before End is pulled through in Step 3 above, make a small Bight in the End with RH.*

6. *Then pull this Bight back through the first Bight. Shoe laces are "double" slipped.*

TWO HALF HITCHES

A quick, easily remembered knot.

Use Securing a line that will not be under great strain, or shake so violently it can come loose. If wet, however, it can jam.

To tie

1. *Proceed through Step 4 in making Half Hitch (page 10).*

2. *With RH pull End up and left over Standing Part. Hold End and Standing Part with left thumb and forefinger.*

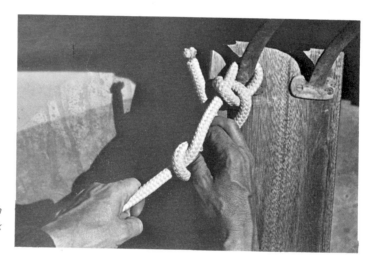

3. *With RH reach through Bight and pull End back through.*

4. *Pull up snug.*

REEF KNOT

This is the same as the Square Knot. It is a general utility knot, quickly made and easily untied.

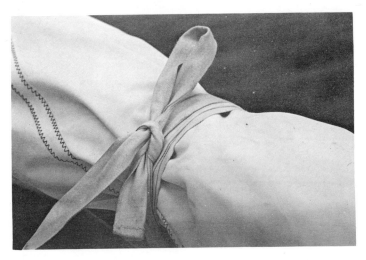

Use   Joining two lines or ends of the same line when strain is *not* great, such as sail gaskets (usually slipped as in illustration), reef points, lashings, etc. Never used for running rigging, as under strain knot may capsize into two reversed Half Hitches and untie itself.

To tie

1. *With first End in RH, cross it over and around second End in LH. Now hold second End in RH and first End in LH. (This is an Overhand Knot—the first step in tying your shoe.)*

2. With RH cross second End behind, up, and around first End. Then tuck through Bight of first End.

3. Pull snug and even. Note—It is important to tie this well-known knot the same way each time. Then when in a hurry you won't tie a Granny by mistake. First over and then behind are the key steps.

To untie

4. Hold Standing Part of one line in LH and the End of the same line in RH.

14

5. *Jerk hands sharply apart to straighten line. Other line now forms two reversed Half Hitches (called a Lark's Head).*

6. *Slip Lark's Head off other line.*

CLOVE HITCH (Crossing Knot)

This hitch is similar to Two Half-Hitches, but a Clove Hitch is made around a Fixed Object, whereas Two Half-Hitches are made back on Standing Part of a line after a Turn is taken around a Fixed Object.

Use   A Crossing Knot to hold a line secure to a series of Fixed Objects such as stanchions. Picture shows a temporary lifeline.

To tie   —Where neither end of Fixed Object is accessible.

1. *With RH pass 12'' end over and around Fixed Object coming up to the right of the Standing Part. Hold Standing Part with LH.*

2. *With RH lead End toward the left over both Standing Part and Fixed Object. Hold crossing with left thumb and forefinger.*

16

3. With RH make another turn around Fixed Object to the left of the first turn.

4. With RH reach down between second turn and Fixed Object and pull End back up.

5. Work knot snug.

CLOVE HITCH (Temporary Hitch)

Use   A quick method of securing a line to a Fixed Object which has an open end such as a bitt or bollard.

To tie

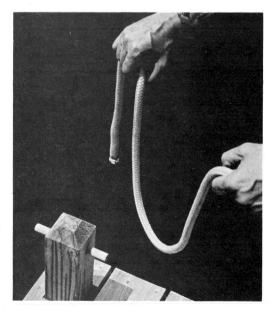

1. *Take Standing Part in LH at point where Hitch is to be made. About 2' Towards End grasp line with RH to make a 2' Open Bight.*

2. With LH cast this Bight over Fixed Object, by bringing Standing Part over Fixed Object to the right with the Bight catching the Fixed Object. RH crosses under LH.

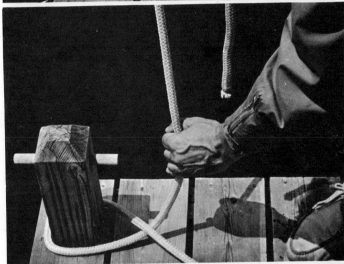

3. With LH pick up End to the right of Standing Part. Slide RH towards Bitter End to make another 2' Open Bight.

4. Move LH to the left back over the Standing Part.

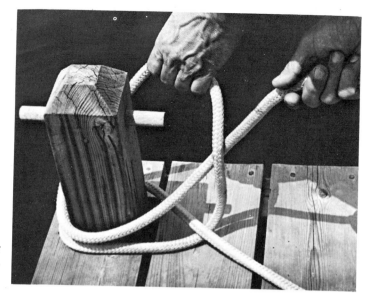

5. *Again with LH cast this Bight over Fixed Object exactly as in Step 2.*

6. *With LH on Standing Part and RH on End, pull snug.*

ROLLING HITCH

An easily adjustable knot when strain is released. It is reasonably secure under strain.

Use Bending one line to another line, the latter being taut. If used to ease or remove the load on the taut line, it is called a preventer. Often used to secure and adjust the length of the tack pendant of the mizzenstaysail or the mainsail jack line as shown in illustration.

To tie

1. *With Standing Part leading from right, hold in LH. With RH take two Turns with End back in direction strain is to be taken. (Practice tying Hitch with strain in either direction.)*

2. *With RH cross End over Standing Part to the left.*

3. *Continuing with RH, and in the same direction as other turns, take a Turn over Fixed Object and tuck End back up through Bight (similar to a Clove Hitch but with one Turn added).*

4. *Adjust to desired position along Fixed Object and pull snug.*

5. *When applying strain, it may be necessary to hold Hitch until it Nips the Fixed Object by twisting it.*

BECKET HITCH

Although the Becket Hitch is sometimes called the Becket Bend and is basically the same knot as the Sheet Bend, it is properly a hitch. The becket is the ring on a block, the bight in the Boltrope of a sail or an eye splice as indicated in the illustration.

23

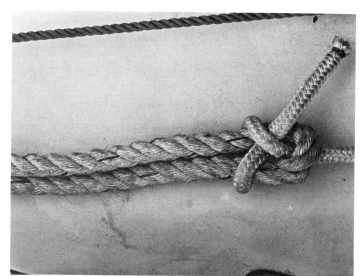

Bending a line to an eye splice

1. With LH hold End of line with eye splice pointing toward you. With RH tuck 8″ End of "tying line" up through eye splice.

2. Continuing with RH through eye, make a Turn with End down over right side of eye, around back of splice, back under left side of eye, and up towards you.

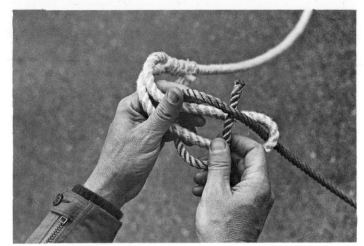

3. *Remove RH from eye and, continuing the Turn, tuck End with RH under Standing Part but over both sides of eye splice.*

4. *Pull up snug.*

5. *When one line is smaller, an extra Round Turn may be added with the tying line for more security. It is then a Double Becket Hitch which also applies to the Sheet Bend.*

STARTING TECHNIQUE FOR TYING CARRICK BEND, SHEET BEND, BOWLINE (Fixed Loop), AND BOWLINE (Fixed Object)

These four knots all begin with the same basic motion which quickly places one line in the Closed Bight of another line. This technique is not easy to picture or describe. Therefore, below are shown photographs of this operation taken with a sequence camera. Once you "see" it from these pictures we are certain you will have no difficulty in mastering it.

The motion is briefly described and illustrated for each knot on the next nine pages. Please note that the Bowline (around a fixed object) is slightly different in that the line is brought *up* against the Standing Part instead of *down* as is the case for the other three knots.

Perform motion with RH. Hold LH still but relaxed.

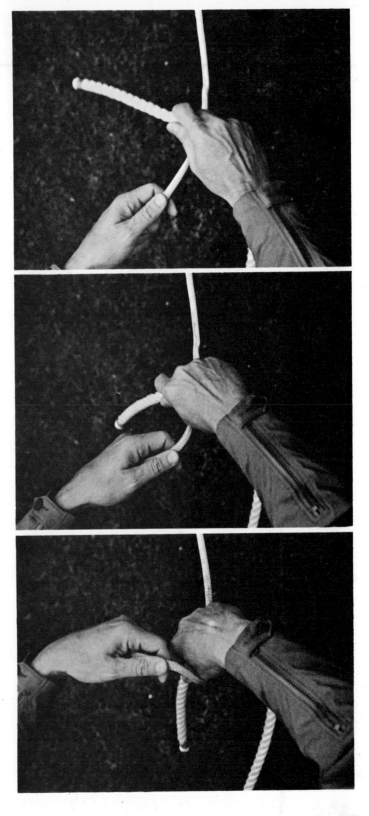

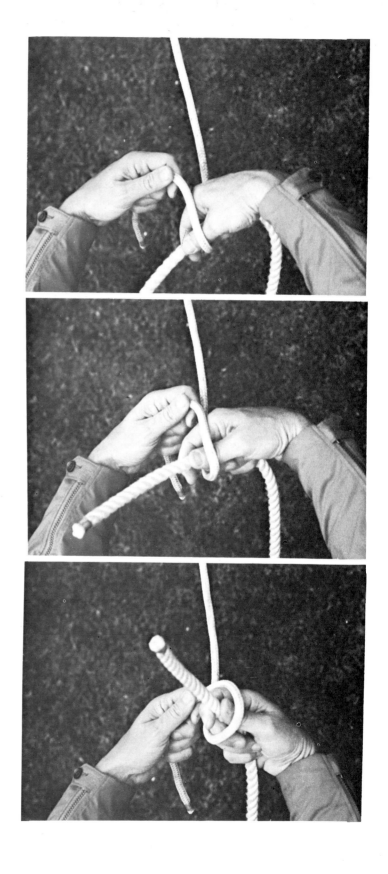

SHEET BEND

Excellent for joining two lines, but not good for maximum loads.

Use   Bending two lines together quickly.

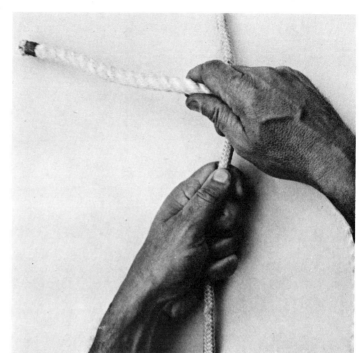

1. With LH hold End of first line pointing toward you. With RH bring 1' End of the second line (pointing away from you) down on Standing Part of first line beyond LH. (The fingers of RH should be just over Standing Part and resting on the first line.)

2. With palm of RH facing down, with one continuous motion rotate right wrist— down, around Standing Part of first line, back toward you

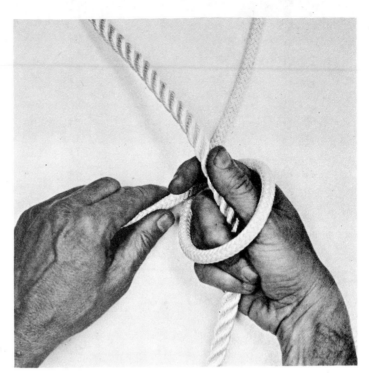

3. *up, and forward again*

4. *finishing with palm up (see more illustrations of this motion on page 26). This forms a Closed Bight in first line with second line up through it, pointing to the right of the first line.*

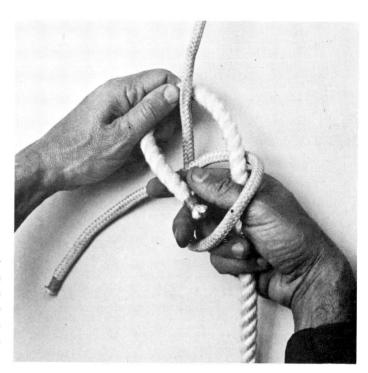

5. With LH reach under Standing Part of first line and pull End of second line back under Standing Part and return to RH, passing it over the cross of the Bight.

6. Move LH to hold Standing Part of first line, and with End and Standing Part of second line in RH, pull snug.

7. If one line is smaller, an extra round turn may be added to make it a Double Sheet Bend. Tie knot with smaller line in left hand adding extra turn after knot is formed as shown in Becket Hitch, Step 5.

BOWLINE (Fixed Loop)

The Bowline (pronounced bo-lin) is the king of knots and is a "must" for all sailors. It can be tied quickly; it is very secure; and it will not jam.

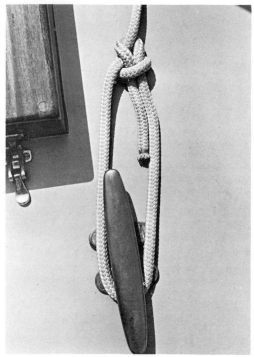

Use   Fixed loop in the end of a docking line. It is often called a Bight.

To tie

1. *Hold Standing Part in LH with 1' End in RH and Open Bight near you. This Bight will form the fixed loop when the knot is tied. Always start to tie this Bowline from this position. Then you will not become confused when tying the Bowline around a Fixed Object (page 36).*

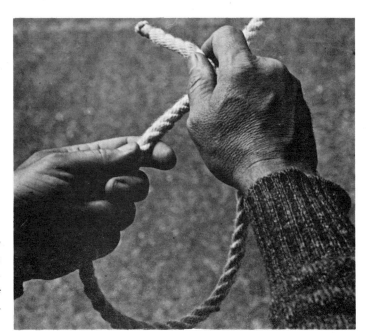

2. With RH bring End (pointing away from you) down on Standing Part beyond LH. (The fingers of RH should be just over Standing Part.)

3. With palm of RH facing down, in one continuous motion rotate right wrist—down, around Standing Part, back toward you, up, and forward again—finishing with palm up (see more illustrations of this motion on page 27).

4. This forms a Closed Bight in Standing Part with fingers of RH in the Bight (palm up), and with the End through the Closed Bight and pointing to the right of the Standing Part.

5. With LH reach under Standing Part and pull End back under Standing Part and return to RH, passing it over the cross of the Bight.

6. *Move LH to hold Standing Part, and with End and right part of fixed loop in RH, pull snug.*

BOWLINE (Around Fixed Object)

Use　Securing a line around or through a Fixed Object. Joining two lines of different sizes requires using this method for bending the second Bowline to the first (see Carrick Bend, page 39).

To tie

1. With LH pass 2' End through or around Fixed Object. Always pass line from left to right (see Step 6). Hold Standing Part in LH near Fixed Object. Hold 1' End, pointing toward you, in RH.

2. With RH bring End up, under Standing Part between your body and LH. (The fingers of RH should be just under Standing Part.)

3. Keep End in RH and rotate, in one continuous motion, right wrist up, then away from you, down through loop and back toward you. End is to the right of the Standing Part (see more illustrations of this motion on pages 26–28). This forms a Closed Bight in Standing Part with RH in Bight.

4. With LH reach over Standing Part and pull End back to the left over Standing Part and return it to RH underneath the cross of the Bight.

5. With Standing Part in LH and with End and right part of fixed loop in RH, pull snug.

6. If after Step 1 you find that you have End in LH by mistake, transfer End to RH under Standing Part. Proceed with Step 2 even though End and Standing Part are crossed. Knot will turn over when strain is applied.

CARRICK BEND

A unique combination of a decorative and very useful knot.

Use   Basis for the Turk's Head which is used in decorating line, stanchions, king spoke of wheel (Illustration A), etc. Best knot for bending two lines of the same or nearly the same size together quickly and securely. Faster than two Bowlines. Illustration B shows knot as usually pictured (see illustration of Step 6 below).

To tie.   —Use two lines of different size for clarity.

1. *With LH hold End of first line (pointing toward you). With RH bring 1' End of second line (pointing away from you) down on Standing Part of first line beyond LH. (The fingers of RH should be just over Standing Part.)*

2. *With palm of RH facing down, in one continuous motion rotate right wrist— down, around Standing Part of first line, back toward you, up, and forward again—finishing with palm up (see more illustrations of this motion on pages 26– 28). This forms a Closed Bight in first line with second line up through it and pointing to the right of the first line.*

3. *Under left thumb and forefinger, hold Bight of first line and End of second line. Move RH down Standing Part of second line about 6".*

40

4. *With RH palm up bring Standing Part of second line clockwise to the left over End of first line, but under LH and End of second line, then over Closed Bight of first line.*

5. *Let go of second line with RH. With RH reach up through Closed Bight and pull End of second line back down through Bight. End must pass over Standing Part of second line where it crosses Bight.*

6. *Hold Standing Part of first line in LH and Standing Part of second line in RH. Jerk hands sharply apart to capsize knot into its working form.*

SINGLE BOWLINE ON A BIGHT

When both ends are secured (or the line is too long to reach its ends), you may sometimes want to make a fixed loop in the line.

Use To make a *secure* fixed loop in Standing Part of a line so that another line can be bent to it.

To tie

1. With LH hold line where you want Bowline. With RH, moving clockwise, make a small Closed Bight. Hold crossing with thumb and forefinger of LH.

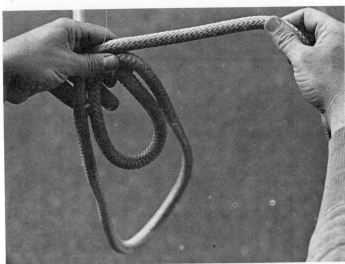

2. Move RH down line and continue clockwise to make a larger second Closed Bight (this forms the fixed loop) around the first Bight. Lay the cross of this second Bight on top of the cross of the small first Bight.

3. Again move RH down line and continue clockwise to make a close Round Turn around small first Bight (but not around fixed loop). Again hold cross of this turn together with the other two crosses with thumb and forefinger of LH.

4. Let go standing part with RH and reach down through small first Bight with RH and pull fixed loop back up through first Bight. Shift LH to Standing Part to release Bights.

5. *Adjust loop to size required. Pull knot snug.*

DRAW HITCH

A temporary Hitch, quickly tied but more quickly untied. Not to be used for loads or security.

Use   Securing a halyard temporarily to a lifeline. Making a dinghy painter fast to pier rail.

To tie

1. This Hitch is really formed from three Open Bights. Make the first Bight about 1' from End. With LH pass Bight under or through Fixed Object. Put fingers of RH back toward you through Bight. Hold Standing Part and End in LH.

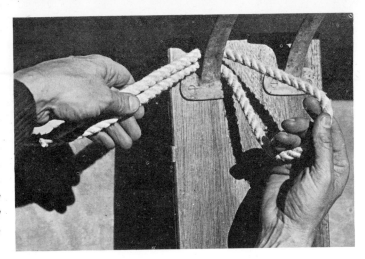

2. Make a small second Bight in Standing Part by reaching through first Bight with RH to pick up Standing Part and pull it back up through first Bight thus forming the second Bight.

3. Letting go Standing Part with LH pull End with LH and second Bight with RH to tighten first Bight around Fixed Object.

4. With RH reach through second Bight to pick up a third Bight in End and pull back through second Bight.

5. Holding third Bight in RH pull Standing Part with LH to tighten. Work Hitch snug and even.

To untie   **6.** Pull End smartly. If desired, when used to secure painter, End can be long enough to be led back to dinghy where it can be pulled to release Hitch.

CONSTRICTOR

Ashley developed this knot for binding. It draws up quickly and will not back off. Sometimes it must be cut to untie unless it is slipped (see page 10).

Use   Quick temporary whipping for the End of a line (Illustration); lashing for battens, tools, etc.; closing for mouth of a ditty bag.

To tie

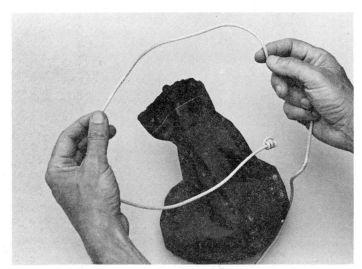

1. *Hold line in both hands about 1' apart. Open Bight away from you.*

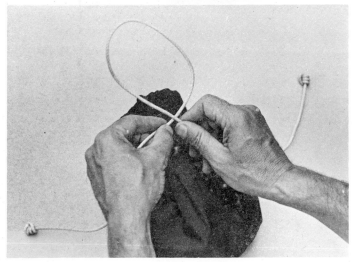

2. *With RH twist (flip) right part over left part to form a Closed Bight. Hold crossing with left thumb and forefinger.*

47

3. With right thumb and forefinger pick up center of Bight. Still with RH, twist Bight so that right side of Bight moves toward you.

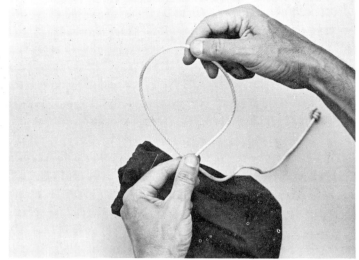

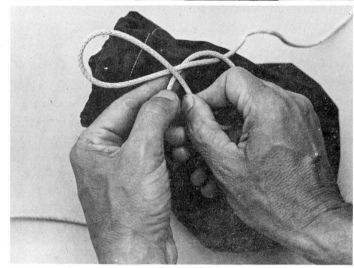

4. Still with RH place center of Bight on top of crossing. Bight now forms two small Closed Bights which look like a "figure eight."

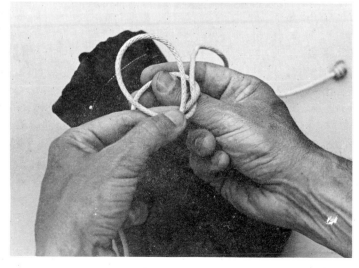

5. With RH fold the nearest Bight down, away from you and up under other Bight.

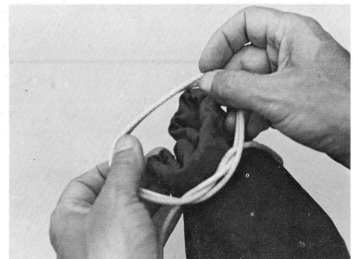

6. *Place Bights over Fixed Object with both hands. Let go with both hands.*

7. *Pull Ends as snug as the use of the knot requires.*

8. *If quick release is desired, knot should be slipped. After Step 4 with RH make a small Open Bight in right End. Then bring right End back to the left under the crossing. This makes a third Bight which is the slip knot. Proceed with Steps 5 and 6. In Step 7 pull left End and third Bight to make knot snug.*

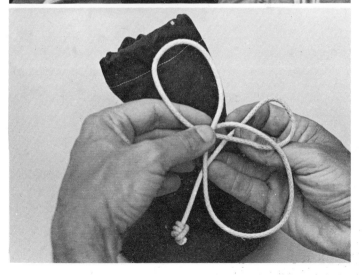

COILS AND FOULED LINES

If you pull either End of the line back through a Bight or Bights, you are probably inadvertently tying Overhand or Figure of Eight Knots in the line, which will have to be untied before the line is used. Putting a strain on a kinked line greatly weakens it. The kink unlays the line so that the surface yarns in each strand are no longer parallel to the axis of a stranded rope. This eliminates the support the three strands give each other.

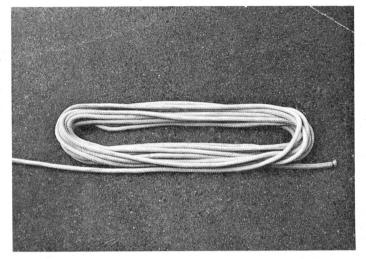

1. *When not in use, lines must be carefully coiled and well secured so that they will run free when needed. A fouled coil is dangerous to ship and crew. Practice making up coils until you are proud of yours.*

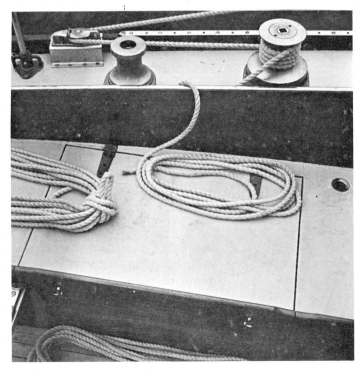

2. *When sheets are in use they are made into coils, but the coils are not made fast. The cockpit sole should be squared away by separating the various coiled sheets and placing them on the deck or seat hatch near their cleat.*

3. When a line to be coiled is lying in a tangled heap, it is cleared by overhauling. Loosen as much as possible by shaking gently.

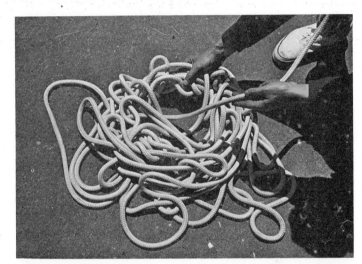

4. Then, without forcing, roll the Standing Part up and out from the center of the tangle.

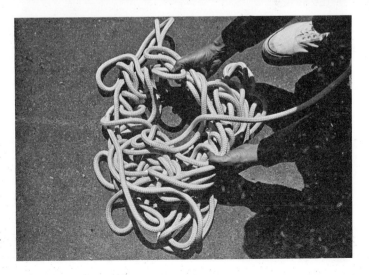

5. Continue to loosen by shaking the fouled parts.

6. *Work Standing Part toward you until line is all cleared.*

MAKING UP A COIL

A line too long or too big to be held in one hand must be coiled on the deck. Cable is left laid—so coil it counterclockwise.

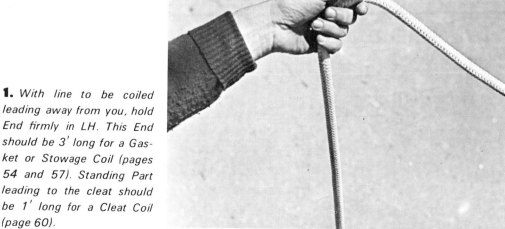

1. *With line to be coiled leading away from you, hold End firmly in LH. This End should be 3' long for a Gasket or Stowage Coil (pages 54 and 57). Standing Part leading to the cleat should be 1' long for a Cleat Coil (page 60).*

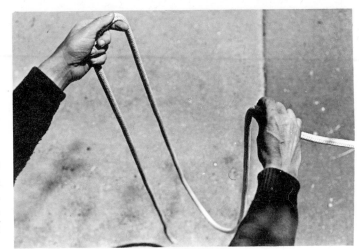

2. *Take Standing Part loosely in RH with Open Bight between hands. Extend both arms fully letting line slide through RH to make the first Bight.*

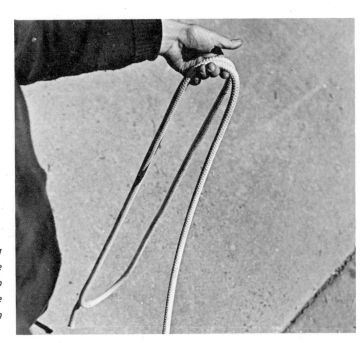

3. *Lower arms, bringing RH to LH and twisting line clockwise with right thumb and forefinger to remove twist from Bight. Take each Bight in LH.*

4. *Repeat Steps 3 and 4 until all line is coiled. Make each Bight the same size, twisting each Bight enough to make it lie fair. If Bights will not lie fair, with each Bight kinking more than the last, don't "fight" it. Uncoil and work out twists in the line along the deck.*

GASKET COIL

The name comes from sailing ships where the gaskets were long and spliced to the yard arm jackstay. Today's gaskets are short and made of sailcloth but the name of the coil remains.

Use A good coil for stowing jib or spinnaker sheets with snap shackles spliced in one end.

1. *Start coil with End which does not have shackle. Then shackle will be available for hook in gear locker. When ready for use, the shackle (the business end) is again available on top of the coil. Coil sheet until 4' or 5' End remains.*

2. *Hold top of coil in RH. About 8" below top, grasp both sides of coil in LH.*

3. *About 6" below top, with RH make Round Turns tightly around coil with shackle End. Work down toward LH. Continue turns until about 2' of End is left.*

4. With RH make a 1' Bight in End. Tuck through eye of coil above Round Turns.

5. With RH pull Bight back over top of coil and down against Round Turns.

6. Pull End to remove Slack and work all parts snug. Cast off by pulling Bight back over top of coil.

7. *In some boats a modified gasket coil may be preferred. In Step 4, instead of tucking Bight through eye of coil, take two more Round Turns. The tuck shackled End through eye of coil. This coil is not so shipshape but is neat enough if shackle is hung on a hook. In racing yachts, this coil may be cast off a few seconds faster.*

STOWAGE COIL

Takes time to make up, but it keeps Bights fair in the coil and thus is neat and shipshape.

Use   Where coil is to be stowed flat with other gear. It is also good for securing mainsheet coil because of its appearance.

1. *Hold coil in LH. With RH make an Open Bight 2' long in End by lifting RH until Bitter End can be grasped by left thumb.*

2. *Drop this Bight behind coil (over left forefinger) and with RH reach through coil and pull Bight back through.*

3. *With RH tuck Bight from right to left under Standing Part of Bight on top of coil. (Lift left forefinger to make way for tuck.)*

4. Drop Bight behind coil again (over left forefinger) and with RH reach through coil and pull Bight back through.

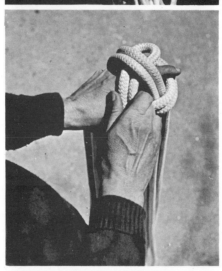

5. With RH tuck Bight from left to right over Standing Part but under last crossing of Bight. (Again use forefinger to make an opening.)

6. With Bight in RH and Standing Part in LH, pull snug. Fair up all Turns, then pull tight.

CLEAT COIL

Quick to make up and easy to cast off.

Use Most often for halyards where cleat is mounted vertically on the mast.

To tie

1. *Hold top of coil in LH with about 8'' of Standing Part between coil and cleat.*

2. With RH reach through coil and pull Standing Part back through coil to form a small Open Bight.

3. With RH hook Bight over top horn of cleat.

4. If coil is not snug against cleat because Bight is too long, unhook Bight and with RH twist counterclockwise to shorten it and rehook.

MAKING FAST TO A CLEAT

A line jammed on a cleat can endanger the boat. It might result in a mast or sail carrying away. The preferred way to make fast for the boat you are in should be ascertained and followed without exception. Then there will be no surprises for the hand who is casting off the line you secured.

In modern boats many cleats are angled about 15° to the lead of the Standing Part. With a "straight" cleat there is a tendency to jam the first Turn against the Standing Part. This is our recommended method to make fast:

1. *Lead line on inside of cleat to far end.*

2. *Take one Round Turn under both horns around outside of cleat. This Turn assists in paying out line slowly under strain.*

3. Cross over center of cleat with one or two Figure of Eight Turns. More Turns are unseamanlike. "Three Half Hitches are more than a king's yacht wants" is an excellent principle for all knot tying.

4. Lines are made fast to a cleat with one Half Hitch —never more. Oddly enough, this simple Hitch can become difficult to tie quickly on a cleat because you may be using either the left or the right horn and you may be using either side of the horn depending on which direction the line was led to the cleat. This means four possible positions for starting the Hitch. The wrong way puts the Standing Part of the Hitch along the side of the cleat and the Nip is weakened, as shown in Number 4, rather than across the cleat, as shown in Number 5.

5. *Make halyards fast with a Half Hitch. Use LH to lead the Standing Part to the same side of the horn as if another Figure Eight Turn were being made. With RH double End back outside Standing Part to form an Open Bight in LH. With LH twist Bight so that End crosses horn under Standing Part. Drop Bight on cleat and pull snug.*

6. *Make sheets or guys fast with a slipped Half Hitch. Use LH to lead the Standing Part to the same side of the horn as if another Figure Eight Turn were being made. With RH double End back inside Standing Part to form an Open Bight in LH. From outside with RH reach across horn under Standing Part and pull back a Bight in the End. Drop Bight in LH on cleat. Pull snug with RH.*

LINE HANDLING ORDERS

It is most embarrassing to hear the command, but not understand what the skipper wants you to do. The better you understand the language of the sea, the more effective a crew member you are.

Here again—"other ships—other customs"—and you can't learn it all at once, but this is a start with some typical orders and their explanations.

1. *To Belay—"Belay mainsheet"—Stop hauling in or paying out and hold or secure temporarily by taking one or more Round Turns without making fast. Also used to request stopping an action.*

2. *To Make Fast—"Make fast jib halyard"—To fasten securely using a Hitch or a Bend.*

3. *To Secure—"Secure boat hook"—To stow or put in place something that is no longer needed. Often used in place of make fast.*

4. *To Let Go—"Let go mizzen sheet"—To ease off or let a line run as far it will go. "Cast off" is close in meaning to "Let go," but more often used with docking lines.*

5. *To Ease—To Start—"Ease the vang six inches"—To pay out slowly a line under stress, but not necessarily to put Slack in it.*

6. *To Take a Strain—'Take a strain on main boom topping lift" —To haul in on a line so that the Slack is taken out of the tackle. The position of the boom, sail or pole should not be changed.*

7. *To Haul—To Heave—"Haul in spinnaker guy"—To pull a line. Heave infers using a winch. Heave is also used to mean throwing a line.*

8. *To Trim—'Trim genny sheet"—Haul in as far as possible or as far as specifically ordered.*

9. *To Overhaul—"Overhaul main sheet"—Clear a tackle so that the lines won't foul in the blocks when a strain is taken. Also to follow the lead of a line such as a spinnaker sheet, to be sure that it is fair in the blocks, lifelines, shrouds, other sheets, etc.*

10. *To Standby—"Standby to jibe"—"Standby to come about"—Get ready to carry out an order, but wait for command to execute.*

11. *"Helm's Alee"—Order to tell crew that the helm, which is delineated by the tiller even though the boat may be rigged with a wheel, is being put "down" to the leeward side of the boat. The bow then comes "up" into the wind. As the boat tacks, the lee sheet is let go, and the weather sheet is heaved in.*

12. *"Helm's Aweather"—Order to tell crew that the helm is being put "up" to the windward side of the boat. Not used so often as "Jibe Oh" since a jibe is probable after the helm is put up. Therefore, "Jibe Oh" is more explicit in relaying the skipper's intention to execute a jibe.*

SHEET WINCHES—GENERAL

All modern winches are geared to take clockwise turns, whether mounted port or starboard. There are many types for various uses: snubbing, top or bottom action, two speed, pedestal, etc. The most common is the top action, to which we will limit our description.

A top action winch has a removable handle which mounts on top of the drum. It is inserted either into a slot (with a spring released catch) or into a square socket (with spring loaded ball checks). Handles must be shoved all the way home so that they are securely locked in place. They are *very dangerous* when they slip, since the arm flies in a wide arc.

A ratchet is built either into the winch itself or the handle so that the handle can be worked back and forth, or it can be rotated 360°. The ratchet is used to "sweat in" the last few inches, using short strokes, while full 360° rotation gets the line in quickly.

The drum will only turn clockwise; so that when paying out a line, the end is slacked off until the turns on the drum slip. This snubbing action permits controlling the amount of line payed out when under heavy strain.

SHEET WINCH—HEAVING IN

Two men usually are detailed to man a sheet winch. The Tail Man to heave in the sheet, and the Handle Man to turn the winch.

1. *The Tail Man decides which cleat he will use which will not interfere with other lines that are now or will soon be in use.*

2. *Tail Man puts two to three clockwise Turns on drum before any strain is taken. Never hand-over-hand a sheet and then expect to take Turns on the winch—a sudden puff and the sail will take charge. The lead of the sheet must be clear to the fairlead block or the cheek block. The snatch block swivel on the track slide must be clear. When ordered, or when clew of jib is clear of the lee shrouds in coming about, the Tail Man takes a strain on sheet by hauling hand-over-hand as fast as possible.*

3. *When the Slack is in, Tail Man snaps on one or two more turns so that line will not slip on winch drum. Tail Man keeps hands more than 2' from winch, keeps the line low enough to clear handle and pulls hard enough to keep line from slipping. After the last Turn goes on, the Handle Man fits the handle as the drum stops turning. Placing his feet to give balance and power, he cranks 360° with both hands (Illustrations 3 and 3A).*

4. When he can't turn freely, he sweats in the last few inches by using his weight to push the handle away from himself, using the ratchet to bring the handle back for another purchase.

5. When sheet is trimmed, Tail Man belays but does not make fast until ordered. Do not use a Half Hitch to make fast unless it is slipped. Sheets can jam under heavy strain. Handle Man unships handle and stows it in its pocket. If no pocket is provided, place it where skipper directs and always put it back in the same place.

6. Tail Man clears end of lee sheet from other lines.

7. Handle Man clears weather sheet, taking two or three Turns on winch. (Step 2 for next tack.) Do not take a strain but take Slack out to be sure sheet is not trailing in the water. No Irish Pennants, please! Wire sheet and guys used on large boats require special handling beyond the scope of this manual.

Safety Reminders   **1.** Hands of Tail Man too close to winch so that handle cuts knuckles; or if line slips, fingers get caught in Turns.

2. Handle is not locked on. It slips and strikes Tail Man.

3. Sheet made fast to a cleat without a slipped Hitch. Squall knocks down boat because sheet cannot be Slacked off quickly because extraordinary strain jammed Half Hitch on horn of cleat.

68

SHEET WINCH—LETTING GO

1. *At command "Standby to come about," make sure end of sheet is still clear and that you are not standing on it or in any of its Bights. Don't get "caught in the Bight of a line."*

2. *Cast Figure of Eight Turns off the cleat, but keep strain on Round Turn so that not a fraction of an inch of sheet pays out. The skipper may change his mind and sail another hour on this tack.*

3. *At command "Helm's Alee," cast off Round Turn from cleat. When jib "breaks" and sheet begins to Slack, quickly free the sheet from the drum by pulling sheet straight up from directly above the winch. Let go sheet.*

4. *Watch sheet to see that it runs free and that the shackle at the clew clears shrouds and mast. If it does foul, sing out "Fouled sheet." The helm may have to be changed to prevent the sail from being torn.*

OVERRIDING TURNS ON A WINCH

Since the drum of a winch will not turn counterclockwise, to pay out the line the Turns must be Slack to reduce the friction. When *either* the Standing Part or the End are allowed to cross over a Turn or Turns, the line will not back off the drum because the friction of the Turns can no longer be reduced.

1. The overriding Turn Nips the Turn or Turns under it by crossing over them.

2. If override is allowed to go too far, the line cannot be heaved in or payed out, because the Standing Part across the top Turn prevents the line from leaving the winch. The winch is useless, and the line cannot be moved either way. In an emergency the line is cut to free it. Jams occur when the lead is poor: (a) too high for the Standing Part leading to the winch, or (b) too low for the End being slacked off.

3. Watch for an overriding Turn. As soon as one starts, heave in or pay out until it clears. Often a jam in the End can be cleared by leading the End counterclockwise back around drum and then to another winch, where strain pulls the Bight in the End under the overriding Turn.

4. When the Standing Part jams so badly it can't be cleared, bend another sheet to the clew if it can be reached. If not, bend a line to the Standing Part of the fouled sheet with a Rolling Hitch. Lead the relieving line to another winch to take the strain off the Standing Part. Then the jam can easily be cleared. NOTE—Never touch any part of the line on the winch until the preventer is rigged and holding.

HALYARD DRUM WINCH—HOISTING WITH DACRON

Top action drum winches are usually used for jib and spinnaker dacron halyards. Tend winch from weather side just forward of the mast looking aft.

To hoist

1. Select cleat with good lead from winch. Make sure halyard is clear aloft— check the head stay. Reeve End through cleat eye and cast in Figure of Eight to secure End.

2. *Cast on two or three clockwise Turns.*

3. *When command to hoist is given, heave in quickly hand-over-hand until halyard is taut.*

4. *Cast on one or two more Turns depending on size of sail.*

5. *Hold halyard in LH and install winch handle with RH. Crank with RH and tail with LH until luff is very taut.*

6. *Make halyard fast on cleat—secure with a Half Hitch. Remove handle and stow it. Coil halyard carefully and secure on cleat.*

HALYARD DRUM WINCH—HOISTING WITH WIRE

For jib and spinnaker *wire* halyards, top action drum winches are usually used. This type of halyard has a dacron tail (about as long as the height of the mast) spliced to the end of the wire so your hands should not touch the wire. Tend winch from weather side just forward of the mast, looking aft.

To hoist Check that, if used, proper length tack and halyard pendants have been bent to jib. If not correct, the splice between dacron tail and wire halyard, after hoisting, will not be between cleat and winch, where it should be. Splice is not strong enough to hold strain above winch, and wire will not bend to secure to small mast cleat.

Select cleat with good lead from winch. Make sure halyard is clear aloft. Check that halyard is clear of head stay. Reeve End of dacron tail through eye of cleat, and cast Figure of Eight in End to secure End (wire forward of mast is heavier than dacron tail and will pull halyard through block at mast head if let go).

1. *Cast on two or three clockwise Turns.*

2. *When command to hoist is given, heave in quickly hand-over-hand until wire starts on drum. Keep hoisting until halyard is taut but add Turns as needed to keep wire from reaching your hands.*

3. *Hold tail in LH and install winch handle with RH. Crank with RH and tail with LH until luff is very taut.*

4. *Make dacron tail fast on cleat—secure with Half Hitch. If wire reaches cleat, add a Turn on winch. Remove handle and stow it.*

75

5. *Coil tail carefully and secure on cleat.*

HALYARD DRUM WINCH
LOWERING WITH DACRON OR WIRE

To lower

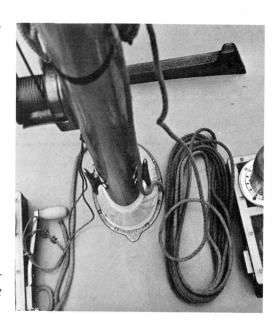

1. *Capsize coil on deck or cabin top with Standing Part leading from top of coil.*

2. *Cast off halyard from cleat. Hold strain on drum so halyard does not back off.*

3. *At command to lower, very carefully remove one or two Turns from drum but leave several to hold halyard from running. Take Turns off by unwinding the end all the way around the drum. Keep the end perpendicular to the drum to prevent all the Turns from jumping off accidentally.*

4. *Ease off the halyard until luff is Slack.*

5. *Cast halyard free from winch and lower handsomely, allowing time for foredeck hand to keep sail out of the water. If sail will fall on deck, halyard may be let go by the run. Remember—When using a drum winch never grasp the wire with your hands when it is under strain. If it runs, your hands will be badly burned.*

77

HALYARD REEL WINCH—HOISTING AND LOWERING

Reel winches hoist wire permanently attached to the drum. They are efficient but devilish, as they have a brake which can slip, and wire is hard to control.

To hoist the mainsail (winch on starboard side of mast)

1. Cast off downhaul which holds gooseneck of boom down to keep proper strain on luff.

2. Insert winch handle securely and hold with LH. With RH release brake.

3. *With RH grasp wire halyard about 2' above winch and pull towards you to remove Slack. With LH on handle take off turns until overriding turns clear. Set brake. Adjust remaining Turns with LH to make them tight and snug.*

4. *With LH reel in halyard slowly. With RH guide halyard, keeping each Turn tight against the last. When weight of sail puts strain on halyard, hoist faster but keep guiding wire. (No danger here of wire slipping to cut your hand as there is with a drum winch.)*

5. *At the end of each layer of wire, keep control of point when direction is reversed. If wire starts back too soon, it will leave an opening for the next layer to sink into. If wire starts back too late, it will build up on itself and jump off. Both situations can cut strands.*

6. When sail is about two Turns from hoisted, pull halyard to one side so it crosses last layer diagonally. This prevents squeezing between two Turns.

7. Hoist until headboard is "two blocked" or measurer's tape on halyard or mast is reached.

8. Secure winch handle.

9. Make sure brake handle is "home."

10. Haul boom down with downhaul to proper set of luff. (See illustration for Step 1 above, page 78).

To lower mainsail   **1.** Make sure topping lift is set up! Don't learn how to "lower the boom" on someone the hard way!

2. Do not use winch handle—it would "windmill" dangerously.

3. At command to lower, release brake. Lower until speed builds up, then brake to a stop. Repeat until sail will not fall by itself. If halyard is let go by the run, it may backlash on the reel and kink the wire.

4. Release brake and pull sail down by hand.

5. Close brake handle.

6. If sail is not to be furled at once, lash head with a gasket to keep a strain on the halyard so it will not foul aloft. Slatting halyards are bad seamanship. With aluminum masts they are noisy, and this is inconsiderate of other boats in the harbor.

BENDING FLAG HALYARD TO FLAGSTAFF

When a flagstaff is used, the flag or pennant (it may be a club burgee, the owner's private signal, a wind sock, or a night hawk) is bent permanently to the end of a staff in such a way that it can rotate. (Actually the flag is bent to a short staff that swivels around the flagstaff.) The halyard is bent to the flagstaff as follows:

1. *Snap ends of halyard to each other or bend them to each other with a Sheet Bend.*

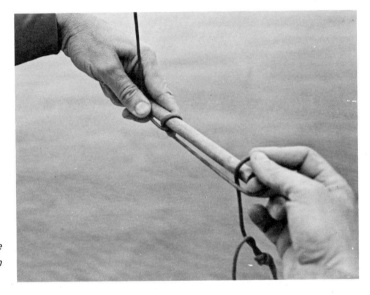

2. *A few inches above the Bend, cast a Clove Hitch on the lower end of the staff.*

3. *Slide Hitch up staff to about 1′ below flag.*

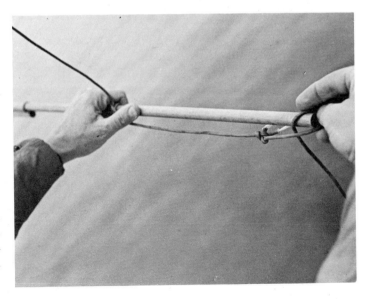

4. *A few inches below the Bend, cast another Clove Hitch onto the staff about 3″ from the end. Pull this Hitch snug.*

5. *Slip first Hitch up staff until Slack is out between Hitches. Top Hitch should not be closer than 6″ to flag. Pull both Hitches tight.*

6. *Hoist slowly, keeping staff horizontal until flag is past backstay.*

7. *On lowering, don't untie Clove Hitches. Simply slide both off lower end of staff. Make halyard fast.*

8. *Don't roll up flag on staff. Stow it flat, or it will take a curl that makes it more difficult to hoist past the backstay in light air.*

PICKING UP THE MOORING

For our purposes, to moor is the act of making a boat fast to a mooring float. When two or more anchors are used in a harbor, a boat is also said to be moored. At the water's surface, most permanent moorings consist of a buoy which supports a heavy mooring cable and a float which supports a light line (pendant) about 10′ long. The latter is bent close to the eye splice in the mooring cable.

1. *The skipper will advise which side of the boat he plans to pick up mooring.*

2. *Get boat hook.*

3. *Clear any lines or sails from foredeck, cleat and bow chocks.*

4. *Guide helmsman as calmly as you can, regardless of impending disaster, to bring rail over float. Do not aim bow at float.*

5. *Hold boat hook so hook is just under water and facing away from bow.*

6. *When hook passes float, dip hook well down into water and swing out catching pendant next to float. As soon as pole hits pendant, pull in.*

7. *If you miss, swing pole back and try again and again.*

8. *When hooked, pull in pole hand-over-hand. Grasp pendant. Place hook on deck.*

9. *Lead pendant under lifeline to mooring cleat. Belay until all way is stopped, and the boat has fallen back with mooring out ahead. Then, haul in mooring eye and drop over on cleat.*

10. *Place cable in chock and bend on chafing gear. Lash eye splice to cleat with pendant by taking Figure of Eight Turns and a Half Hitch.*

HEAVING A LINE

A heaving line is technically a braided line with a rope covered weight (a monkey fist) bent to one end. On the auxiliary a long docking line, even two lines bent together, is most often used.

1. *Make one end fast to a cleat; lead line outboard and up and back over lifelines. Put large Bowline in other end if monkey fist or eye splice is not used.*

2. *Coil all the line into LH with about 2' Bights.*

3. *Divide coil in half, with LH holding Standing Part half, and RH holding half to be heaved, with about 4' of Slack between coils.*

4. *When you know the line will be long enough to carry to objective, open fingers of LH so Bights will pay out one by one.*

5. *Using RH coil as a weight, heave it sidearm and underhand, aiming over the head of the man receiving the line. Bights in RH coil should stay together until they have pulled all the line from LH.*

6. *If line is missed, quickly recoil to keep it clear of propeller. Divide coil and heave again.*

7. *When dockhand has line in hand, ask him to drop Bowline or eye splice over cleat or pile. Then you, not he, control how much to haul in. Enthusiastic line handlers ashore often haul in too short too quickly. The skipper may wish to back down on the full scope of the line, depending on wind, tide, and other boats.*

DOCKING LINES

When a vessel is docked, it lies alongside a float or pier. Technically the water is the dock (therefore drydock). The lines used to secure the boat are docking lines, but often they are called mooring lines. They are about 25' long, usually with an eye splice in one end. The principal docking lines are:

1. *Bow Line—Leads from the inboard bow chock ahead to the pier.*

2. *Stern Line—Leads from the outboard stern chock astern to the pier.*

3. *Breast Lines—Lead at right angles to the keel from the rail to the pier. There can be a Bow Breast, Waist Breast, and Quarter Breast. Breast lines, when led to a pier as opposed to a float, may go Slack or taut between ebb and flow of the tide and must be tended regularly.*

4. *Spring Lines—Lead fore or aft alongside the boat. The After Bow Spring or the Forward Quarter Spring (Illustration) should be at least as long as the boat but a minimum of three times the height of the tide. They prevent the boat from moving ahead or astern as the tide ebbs and flows or the wind changes. Docking lines should be tended from the boat, not the pier. (See Heaving A Line, page 86, paragraph 7.) If short handed when leaving a berth, make one end of each docking line fast on deck, send other end ashore around a bollard or cleat or through a ring or the eye of a cleat, then back on board to a cleat. Then lines may be cast off with no help from the float or pier.*

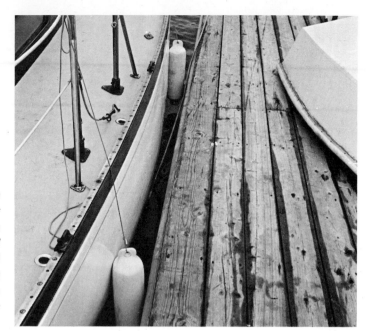

5. *After studying where the side of the boat will bear on the pier, place fenders accordingly. Use a slipped Clove Hitch (Crossing Knot) to secure the fender pendant to the lifeline, but reeve the end through the Bight for security.*

6. *If your line must go on the same cleat or bollard as the line of another boat, run your Bowline or Bight up through his Bight and then drop over bollard. Either line may then be cast off without disturbing the other.*

THE YACHT'S TENDER

The small boat (the tender) used primarily to go back and forth from a pier or float to a yacht on a mooring, may be a flat bottom row boat, a larger pulling boat, a motor boat, an inflatable life raft or a dinghy. Since the 8′ or 9′ fiberglass dinghy is by far the most prevalent on sailing yachts, the discussion on line handling for tenders is limited to this type.

1. *Securing alongside.*

Most yachts have a gate in the lifelines on the starboard side. When coming alongside to deliver passengers and supplies it is often convenient to secure the *"dink"* temporarily to the lifeline with a draw hitch. (See Page 44). If the painter is about 15′ long the end may be led back aboard the dinghy.

When the oarsman is ready to shove off for the next load he does not have to reach precariously over the dinghy's unstable bow to let go (especially in a current). After seated and ready to row he simply pulls the end of the painter to capsize the draw hitch.

If the dinghy is to be left unattended, secure painter to a cleat or with a bowline.

2. *Securing to a mooring pendant.*

With the pendant made fast to the yacht's bow cleat, lead the painter inboard under the bow pulpit. If the painter is short, make it fast to the mooring pendant bight with a bowline. If it is long, double the painter and pass it through the bight using the doubled line to make a normal bowline.

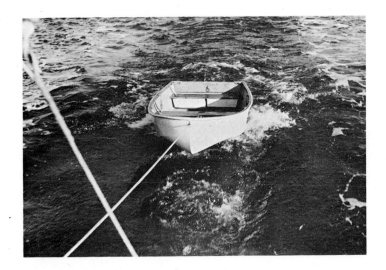

3. *Towing astern.*

(A) *Under Power*

The tender offers the least drag when towed on the forward side of the first stern wave in the wake. In this position the dinghy's bow is supported by the painter and its stern planes downhill on the forward edge of the wave. There is a minimum of wetted surface and, in good weather, no yawing.

91

In moderate following seas the dinghy should be towed on the forward side of the second or third wave. If towed too closely, it may charge up, ramming the stern. In bad weather, the dinghy will be on board, lashed down.

A right hand propeller tends to drive the ship's head to port and, although it will not balance completely, it does compensate somewhat to tow from the chock on the starboard quarter.

(B) *Under Sail*

Usually the wake is not large enough to make much difference and the scope of the painter is increased to 50' or more, trying to find the forward side of a wave. Lengthening the painter cushions yanking the dinghy. The carrick bend should be used to lengthen the painter. It can be soaked for days under strain, yanked repeatedly and can still be untied with ease.

4. *Hoisting aboard.*

When preparing to race, strong hands manhandle the dinghy aboard in seconds but women should not be asked to reach over lifelines to pick up even one end of the dinghy.

Properly prepared, one man can bring the dinghy aboard quite easily using the main halyard. If a special bridle is not available, a sufficient one can be quickly rigged with the painter. Lead it aft from the bow of the dinghy. Above the midship thwart, cast in a single bowline on a bight, leaving a small loop. (See Page 34). Continue the painter aft through the stern ring and adjust the length with a rolling hitch. If there is no stern ring, lead the painter through the port and starboard seat brackets and then put the rolling hitch (See Page 20) on the standing part. Secure the main halyard shackle to the bowline. Detail a hand to heave in on the halyard while you fend off as the dinghy comes over the lifelines.

Place two small fenders along the inboard edge of the grab rail, then lower away until dinghy rests between the cabin house and the lifelines. Slack the main sheet and secure the boom out of the way. Taking hold of the stern of the dinghy, capsize it onto its chocks. Secure the dinghy, using the two gripes fitted for the purpose or use a length of line criss-crossing from the bows to the opposite quarters.

GLOSSARY

Many of these terms have several meanings. Only the one or ones pertinent to this manual are given. The page number in parenthesis refers to that use of the term in the text which best illustrates it; words in italic may be found elsewhere in the Glossary.

ABAFT   Toward or in the stern, adverb; see *mizzenstaysail*.

AFT, AFTER-   Toward or in the stern, adverb or adjective; see *forward*. (p. 88)

BACKSTAY   A *stay* to keep a *mast* from leaning (raking) forward. Can be either fixed or running. Running *backstays* are rigged on both sides of the boat and are set up or slacked off depending on the point of sailing. (p. 82)

BATTEN   Narrow, thin piece of wood or plastic inserted in a pocket in the *leech* of a sail to stiffen it. (p. 47)

BECKET   A loop of rope or an *eye* to which a line may be secured. (p. 23)

BELAY, TO   See Line Handling Orders, page 65. (p. 68)

BEND   A knot joining two lines. (p. 29)

BEND, TO   To tie two lines together or to tie a line to a *Fixed Object* (often using a *Hitch*), or to secure a sail to a boom or stay ready for hoisting. (p. 2)

BIGHT   See Basic Terms, page 3. (p. 33)

BITT(S)   A square post or pair of posts with or without a crossbar (norman) for securing heavy lines. Usually in the bow of a boat. (p. 5)

BITTER END   Technically the inboard *end* of the anchor *rode*. It was originally the *end* secured to the *bitts*. We use it as defined on page 3. (p. 19)

BLOCK   A pulley. There are many kinds—single, double, snatch, *cheek*, etc. The line runs over the *sheave* set between the two shells (*cheeks*) of the *block*. (p. 65)

BOLLARD   A round heavy post for securing lines. Sometimes on a boat, but usually on a pier. (p. 88)

BOLTROPE   *Rope* sewn in the edge of a sail. (p. 2)

BURGEE   A flag indicating the yacht club of the owner, flown at the main *truck* (*fore truck* on a schooner). It may be pointed or swallowtailed. (p. 81)

BY THE RUN   To let go a line completely without slowing the speed it runs out; see *pay out*. (p. 77)

CABLE   Technically three *ropes laid up* left handed. In modern practice any large line—usually used for anchoring; see *rode*. Chain is also called cable. (p. 52)

CAPSIZE, TO   To turn over a coil from the position it was stowed so that the *standing part* will run free. To turn over parts of a knot. (p. 41)

CAST IN, TO To put a knot or splice in a line. (p. 74)

CAST OFF, TO To take *Turns* off a winch or *bitt*, etc. May imply hauling the line in after casting off, as is the case with docking lines. (p. 62)

CAST ON, TO To put *Turns* on a winch or *bitt*, etc. (p. 72)

CHAFING GEAR Any device—leather, rope, plastic, etc.—to prevent lines, sails, decks, or *spars* from wear. (p. 85)

CHEEK BLOCK *Block* with only one shell. The other shell is formed by the rail, *spar* or deck to which it is permanently fitted. It may also be a *snatch block*. (p. 6, USE picture)

CHOCK Device to hold a line in place as it passes over or through the rail. (p. 85)

CLEAT A fitting made of wood, brass, or iron for making lines fast; see *horns*. (p. 60)

CLEAT EYE A hole in the center of some *cleats* for securing the *Bitter End* of the line being used so that it will not come adrift. (p. 71)

CLEW The lower *after* corner of the sail. (p. 67, picture of jib)

COCKSCOMBING Various methods of fancy work with small stuff to dress up rails, *stanchions*. (p. 1)

COME ABOUT, TO See *to tack*. (p. 65)

DOWNHAUL A *tackle* fitted to the boom *gooseneck* to keep a proper strain on the *luff*. (p. 78)

END See Basic Terms, page 3.

EYE SPLICE A *Bight* (fixed loop) formed in the *end* of a line by splicing the end back into its *Standing Part*. (p. 23)

FAIR, TO To put the parts of a knot in their proper positions. To arrange the *Bights* in a coil so they lie in order. (p. 54)

FAIRLEAD A device—*block*, *chock*, etc.—to keep a line in a desired position so that it will not foul other gear and will not chafe. (p. 71, picture, Step 4)

FIXED OBJECT See Basic Terms, page 4.

FOOT Lower edge of a sail. (p. 21, USE picture)

FOOTROPE A line stretched beneath the yards of a ship on which men stand when sail handling. (p. 2)

FORWARD, FORE- (Pronounced forrard) Toward or in the bow. (p. 88)

GASKET A short piece of sailcloth or line used to furl the sails on their booms. (p. 13, USE picture)

GENOA JIB (Genny) Very large jib extending well *aft* of the *mainmast*. (p. 65)

GOOSENECK Fitting which holds the boom to the mast. (p. 78)

GRANNY A Reef Knot incorrectly tied since the "second step," page 13, is reversed. It is *not* reliable.

GRIPES Broad straps used to secure a boat to the davits or on decks. (p. 93)

GUYS Lines, sometimes wire, to control the position of a *spar*. The *spinnaker* pole has two; the *after guy* usually led to a *snatch block* on the *quarter*, and the *fore guy* led to a *fairlead block* at the bow. (p. 64)

HALYARD Line, often wire, used to hoist and lower a sail or flag. (p. 81)

HAND-OVER-HAND To haul in a line rapidly when it is not under strain. (p. 75)

HANK Brass catch or snap hooks on the *luff* of a jib used to *bend* the sail to the *forestay*; see *jackline*. Also used as a verb; see *set flying*.

HANDSOMELY Deliberately, slowly, with control. (p. 77)

HAUL, TO See Line Handling Orders, page 65.

HEAD The uppermost part of a triangular sail (jib-*headed*). The headboard is sewn in the *head* and takes the strain of the *halyard*. The bow of the boat is called the *head* when referring to the direction the boat is going (heading). (p. 80)

HEAVE, TO See Line Handling Orders, page 65.

HELM The *helm* controls the direction of the boat by means of the rudder. One "takes the *helm*" when he assumes charge of the tiller or the wheel. (p. 65)

For hundreds, if not thousands, of years the tiller's position has indicated the *helm's* position. If the *helm* (tiller) was put to port the boat's *head* went to starboard and vice versa. When the wheel replaced the tiller several hundred years ago, it was rigged to work like a tiller—wheel (*helm*) turned to port and the boat's *head* went to starboard. This was confusing on a steamship, and the wheel's rigging was gradually changed to operate as an automobile now does— wheel turned to port and the *head* went to port. By World War II, all vessels, whether sail or power, were changed so that the *head* moved in the same direction as the wheel. "Starboard *helm*" and "Port *helm*" were officially forbidden, and the typical orders to the *helm* are now "Left rudder" or "Right rudder," "Come left 20°," "Come right 15°," etc.

The beginner should understand that the orders *to the helmsman—* not the *helm*—to "Come up," "Come higher," "Come closer," mean he should alter the *helm* so as to sail closer to the wind. "Come down," "Come away," "Fall off," mean for him to alter the *helm* to sail further from the wind. Don't use *"Helm up"* or *"Helm down,"* even though technically correct.

HITCH A knot used to *bend* a line to a *spar*, ring, or other line. (p. 8)

HORNS The two arms or projections of a *cleat*. (p. 62)

IRISH PENNANT A line or part of the rigging which has come adrift and is hanging loose in an unseamanlike fashion. (The *weather* jib *sheet* is a common offender.) (p. 68)

JACK LINE A line which when taut holds the lower part of the *luff* of a large sail close to the track slides or jib *hanks* when the sail is hoisted. On the mainsail it is fitted to permit roller reefing. (p. 21)

JACK STAY A wire *rope* or rod running along the top or bottom of the *spars* of a ship to which the sails are *bent*. (p. 54)

JIBE, TO With wind astern, a shift of a sail from one side of boat to the other (can be violent if not controlled). It can be caused by change in course to bring wind across *leech* of sail or by change in direction of wind. (p. 65)

LAID UP See *strand*. (p. 1)

LEAD (Rhymes with seed.) As a noun: the way in which a line runs between two points. It should be unobstructed. As a verb: "*Lead* jib *sheet* outboard of *shrouds*." (p. 62)

LEECH The *after* edge of a sail. (p. 2)

LEECH LINE A small line *rove* through the hem of the *leech* whose adjustment controls the shape of the sail and excessive flutter.

LEE, LEEWARD (Pronounced Loo-ard) Away from the wind. A *lee* shore can portend disaster for a sailboat. (p. 67)

LIFELINES Permanent lines rigged to keep the crew aboard in bad weather; or for small children, temporary ones are set up. (p. 16)

LIFT The line, rigged from a mast, which holds the outboard end of bosom or *spinnaker* pole in desired horizontal position. Often it is called the pole *lift* or *topping lift*. (p. 80)

LUFF The *forward* edge of a sail. (p. 2)

MAKE FAST, TO See Line Handling Orders, page 65. (p. 63)

MANROPE The several lines hanging down to a lifeboat. These are knotted at intervals to prevent the men from slipping. Also ropes on gangways. (p. 2)

MAST When combined with the name describing it, such as mainmast, foremast, etc., mast is pronounced "*must*"; see mizzenstaysail.

MEASURER'S TAPE When a boat is measured to calculate her rating for racing, the measurer may put a band of tape at the limits to which a sail may be set. (p. 80)

MIZZENSAIL A *fore* and *aft* sail set on the mizzen or *after mast* of a yawl or ketch. It has a boom. (p. 65)

MIZZENSTAYSAIL A *fore* and *aft* sail whose *luff* is *set flying* from the mizzenmast *truck forward* to the deck *abaft* the mainmast. The *sheet leads* to the *mizzen* boom. (p. 21)

MONKEY FIST A small weight covered with a rope knot, similar to a *Turk's Head*. *Bent* to a *heaving* line, it has enough mass when thrown to pull the line behind it. (p. 85)

NIGHT HAWK   A small, long dark *pennant* flown only at night in place of the club *burgee* and the *private signal*. (p. 81)

NIP   See Basic Terms, page 4. (p. 63)

OUTHAUL   A *purchase*, either a *tackle* or small wire reel winch, to pull the *clew* of a sail *aft* along a boom.

OVERHAND KNOT   A simple knot which will not hold by itself. (p. 8)

OVERHAUL, TO   See Line Handling Orders, page 65. (p. 51).

PAINTER   A short, small line secured to the bow of a small boat for towing or *making fast*. (p. 46)

PAY OUT, TO   To let go or slack off a line. It infers that the rate is controlled. (p. 62)

PEDESTAL WINCH   A winch used on larger sailboats. The handles are mounted on a pedestal above the deck so that one or two men can operate the winch while standing up. (p. 66)

PENDANT   (Pronounced pennant) A short line permanently spliced to an object for quick hauling—center board *pendant*, mooring *pendant*, etc., or a short wire line used to position a sail such as a *tack pendant*. (p. 82)

PENNANT   A flag whose fly is longer than its hoist; used to signify a special situation, i.e., Answering *Pennant*, Numeral *Pennant*, etc. (p. 81)

POINT   One of 32 points of the compass. As verb, to sail close to the wind.

PREVENTER   A line rigged to give extra support to another line or to hold another line under strain. (p. 71)

PRIVATE SIGNAL   A flag specially designed to identify a yacht's owner (p. 81)

PULPIT   A permanent life rail supported by stanchions. They are found on both the bow and stern.

PURCHASE   A *tackle* or device used to increase hauling power.

QUARTER   The boat's side, either port or starboard, from amidships *aft* to the stern. (p. 88)

REEF POINTS   Small lines *rove* through grommets set in the sail on lines parallel to the *foot* and used to reef the sail. (p. 13)

REEVE, TO   (past tense ROVE) To run the end of a line through a *fairlead* or *block*, or any opening; see *tuck*. (p. 71)

RODE   A name applied to the anchor line or *cable* whether of *rope* or chain. (p. 1)

ROPE   Cordage over one inch in circumference (about the size of a pencil). It may be twisted or braided, having organic or synthetic fibers, or wire; see *strand*. (p. 2)

LINES CALLED ROPES

1. BACKROPE—the lines, most often chain, rigged from the dolphin striker to the bow.

2. BELL ROPE—the line bent to the clapper.

3. BREASTROPE—the line supporting the leadsman in the chains.

4. BUCKET ROPE—the line bent to the bail of the bucket.

5. DIP ROPE—the line used to clear the hawse or move one hawser under or over another.

6. FOOTROPE—the line, usually of served wire, rigged to a yard arm supported by stirrups for the hands to stand on.

7. TOPROPE—the line used to hoist and lower topmast.

8. MANROPE—lines used on gangways and ladders as a hand hold.

9. YARD ROPE—lines used to lower or raise the yard to or from the deck—not to be confused with the lift that supports the yard when it is rigged.

10. BOLTROPE—the line sewn in the edges of a sail to give support to the robands, track slides, or line bending sail to a boom or a gaff.

ROUND TURN   See Basic Terms, page 5.

RUNNING RIGGING   All lines and gear used to set and trim sails; see *standing rigging*. (p. 13)

SAIL   When combined with the name describing it, such as Mainsail, Foresail, etc., sail is pronounced "sul." (p. 78)

SCOPE   The amount of anchor *cable* in use in relation to the depth of the water. The amount of *Slack* in a line, especially a docking line. (p. 87)

SECURE, TO   See Line Handling Orders, page 65. (p. 62)

SET FLYING, TO   To set a sail by pulling the *luff* taut instead of *hanking* the *luff* to a *stay*. The sail "flies" while it is in the process of being set, since it has no *stay* to hold or guide it; see *spinnaker*.

SHACKLE   A small U-shaped fitting often used to join the *thimble* in an *eye splice* to a fitting. The open end is connected by a screw pin. (A snap *shackle* has a spring loaded pin.) (p. 55)

SHEAVE   (Pronounced shiv) The roller in a *block* over which the line passes; see *block*.

SHEET   Any line or wire *rope* attached to the lower, *after* corner of a sail (or boom) for the purpose of trimming or setting it. The *spinnaker sheet* is the line secured to the *clew*, which is the opposite corner to the one made fast to the pole; see *guy*. (p. 66)

SHROUD   Wire rope supporting a mast laterally, usually from the *truck* to the rails. It is set up by rigging screws (turnbuckles); see *stay*. (p. 69)

SLACK   See Basic Terms, page 5. (p. 65)

SLATTING   Slack lines (especially *halyards*) beating against a *mast* or *spar*. (p. 80)

SNATCH BLOCK   Single *block* with a latch in one *cheek*. When open, the *Bight* of a line may be put in the *block* without *reeving* the *End*. (p. 67)

SNUB, TO   To hold or check a line which is running. Usually done by a *Turn* or *Turns* around a *cleat*, winch or *bitt*. (p. 66)

SNUBBING WINCH   A winch with no handle. It idles when *heaving* in but holds by friction when *paying out* since the rachet prevents the drum from reversing; see *snub*. (p. 66)

SOLE   The "floor" or deck of the cockpit or cabin. The "floors" in a boat are the thwartship timbers connecting the frames. (p. 50)

SPAR   In general, any mast, yard, pole or boom. (p. 2)

SPINNAKER   A light, very large, three-cornered sail *set flying forward* of all *fore stays*. It is set when the wind is free—for running or *reaching*. (p. 74)

SQUARE AWAY, TO   The act of arranging or stowing the gear in a shipshape fashion. Also, to change course to sail before the wind. (p. 50)

STANCHION(S)   The upright posts, usually stainless steel, supporting the *lifelines* and pulpit rails. (p. 16)

STANDING PART   See Basic Terms, page 3.

STANDING RIGGING   All lines and gear used to support the masts; see *running rigging*.

STAY   Wire *ropes* supporting a mast or bowsprit *fore* and *aft*. They are set up with turnbuckles (rigging screws) or *block* and *tackle;* see *shroud*. (p. 71)

STOPPER   A short line used to hold another line, or to control it while *paying out*. (p. 6)

STRAND   *Yarns* twisted together form a strand. *Strands* twisted together (*laid up*) make *rope*. (p. 50)

TACK   The lower, *forward* corner of a sail. (p. 21)

TACK, TO   To *come about;* to bring the wind from one side to the other by turning boat into and through the wind. (p. 55) Port *tack*—Wind blowing on port side of boat. Starboard *tack*—wind on starboard side of boat. (p. 69)

TACKLE   (Pronounced tay-kill) Also called *block* and *tackle*. A means of gaining leverage by a line *rove* through one or more blocks; usually two or more. The number of lines which support the load determine the mechanical advantage; see *purchase*. (p. 65)

TAIL   A short synthetic *rope* spliced to the end of a wire *rope* (usually a *halyard*) to make handling and securing the wire easier. The tail splice will run through a *block* whereas an *eye splice* would not. (p. 74)

TAIL, TO   To haul on a line being *heaved* in by a winch. *Tailing* provides the friction which keeps the line from slipping on the drum. (p. 66)

THIMBLE Metal ring or eyelet around which a line is spliced. The line fits into the concave outside. The convex inside bears the strain and wear; see *shackle*.

TOPPING LIFT A line rigged to support a boom. (p. 65)

TRUCK The top of a *mast*. Often it is a flat, round cap fitted with *sheaves* to carry *halyards;* see *mizzenstaysail*.

TUCK, TO In knot tying, inserting the end of the line between two other lines or two parts of the same line. In splicing, inserting a *strand* between two other *strands*. (p. 7)

TURK'S HEAD A knot used for decoration, to keep hands or feet from slipping on a line, and to finish off the *Ends* of the *strands* in a splice. (p. 39)

TURN See Basic Terms, page 5.

TWO BLOCKED A *tackle* which has been *hauled* short so that the *blocks* touch. Also, refers to *running rigging* (particularly *halyards*) which has been hoisted as far as possible. (p. 80)

UNLAY To unwind the *strands* of a rope. Usually in order to work in a splice. (p. 50)

VANG A temporary *tackle* used to hold a boom or gaff in a particular position.

WAIST The midship part of a boat. (p. 88)

WEATHER See *windward*. (p. 65)

WHIPPING *Round Turns* made with small stuff on the *End* of a line to prevent it *unlaying*. (p. 47)

WIND SOCK A cylindrical bunting hoisted on a flagstaff. It is free to rotate to indicate the direction of the wind. (p. 81)

WINDWARD (Pronounced . winnerd) Toward the wind. Direction wind is blowing from. The weather (*windward*) side of the boat. A *windward* shore gives protection. (p. 65)

YARN Long fibers twisted together; see *strand*. (p. 50)

CONCLUSION

This is intended to be a working manual for beginners. Sailing is an art, however, so although we have made many dogmatic statements we realize that they are merely opinions. If you disagree with us, please advise us of our errors, and we will follow the old sailor's command, "Stand clear, ground swell, while a deep sea rolls by."

ACKNOWLEDGMENT

The following books have been of real value in preparing this manual. They are highly recommended for further study of knots and lines.

Ashley, Clifford W. *The Ashley Book of Knots*, Garden City, N. Y.: Doubleday & Co., Inc., 1944.

Smith, Harvey Garrett. *The Arts of the Sailor*, Princeton, N. J.: D. Van Nostrand Co., Inc., 1953.

The Marlinspike Sailor, Tuckahoe, N.Y. John de Graff Inc., 1970

Day, Cyrus Lawrence. *The Art of Knotting and Splicing*, Annapolis, Maryland: U.S.S. Naval Institute, 1964.

Graumont and Hensel. Encyclopedia of Knots and Fancy Rope Work. Cambridge, Maryland: Cornell Maritime Press, 1953.

Gibson, Charles E. *Handbook of Knots and Splices*, New York: Emerson Books, Inc., 1963.

Boatswain's Mate 3 & 2, Nav. Pers. 10121-D, Washington, D. C.: U. S. Government Printing Office, 1964.

The majority of the photographs were taken by Christa Doertenbach Bennett. Several were taken by Peter Renngli and by Alex Walter.